THE ANCIENT ROMAN ART

ART HISTORY BOOKS FOR KIDS
Children's Art Books

Speedy Publishing LLC
40 E. Main St. #1156
Newark, DE 19711
www.speedypublishing.com

Copyright © 2017

All Rights reserved. No part of this book may be reproduced or used in any way or form or by any means whether electronic or mechanical, this means that you cannot record or photocopy any material ideas or tips that are provided in this book

In this book, we're going to talk about the history of Ancient Roman art. So, let's get right to it!

Roman art wasn't just the art that originated from Rome. Instead, the term **"Roman art"** describes art from the entire civilization of the Roman Empire. Roman art covers a time period of over 1,000 years from the founding of Rome by Romulus and Remus to the reign of the Emperor Constantine.

Details of Romulus and Remus on the Allegory of Tiber.

Face of the Emperor Constantine and Coliseum.

Art flourished throughout the centuries and was often used to honor the memory of specific leaders or battles. The Romans had a tendency to absorb the best of the cultures around them and also the cultures of countries they conquered. They refined the work that the earlier cultures had done.

Many of the features of Roman art come from the culture that preceded them—the Etruscans. The Romans had conquered the Etruscans in March of 509 BC.

As the Romans began to spread through the lands of Italy, regions of Europe, and across the Mediterranean, they learned about the Etruscan styles of art. They absorbed the Etruscan styles including the architecture of temples and the characteristics of sculpture as well as wall painting and portraits.

Colosseum in Rome and morning sun, Italy.

THE ROMANS IMITATED THE GREEKS

The Romans truly admired the culture that the Greeks had created. They were especially intrigued by the Grecian statues. After Rome conquered Greece, they brought Greek artists to the city of Rome so that they would create sculptures for new Roman buildings. The Romans quickly soaked up all that the masters of Grecian art could give to them.

Grecian civilization and the culture of the Greeks had spread to the south of Italy as well as to Sicily, because of the Greek colonies situated there. Plutarch, who wrote during the 2nd century AD, stated that before Rome had conquered Greece, the city was filled to the brim with bloody bodies and barbaric weapons. The culture of Greece brought an air of refinement that hadn't been seen in Rome before.

Tragic mask in hand of greek statue of Melpomene.

After the Romans sacked Corinth in 146 BC, the spoils of the captured Greek treasures began to arrive in Rome. Hellenistic art was admired by the Romans who generally had a stricter demeanor and appearance than the Greeks. It took more than 250 years before Grecian art was fully accepted. This happened during the reign of Emperor Hadrian from 117 AD to 138 AD.

Socrates statue.

During the later republic period as well as the early imperial period, artists were brought from Greece to Rome. They were commissioned to create the plans and designs for buildings as well as to repair important sculptures and make new sculpture creations.

Roman Forum.

The Romans were gradually absorbing the art techniques and principles in this Hellenistic culture they had conquered. They studied the Greek statues and eventually copied them on their own, although they preferred to work in marble than bronze. Roman artists also copied the portrait bust and made it more realistic than those that the Greeks had created.

The portrait bust became very popular. Prosperous Romans would have busts of their influential ancestors created. They would place these in the front atriums of their dwellings to show off their heritage and lineage.

Etruscan Painting

OTHER INFLUENTIAL CULTURES

The Greek culture had the most influence on Roman art, but other cultures influenced Roman art as well. As the Romans conquered other countries and came in contact with other cultures, these cultures were an influence on Roman art. The ancient art of the Egyptians as well as art created by the Germans and the Celts all had some influence on Roman art.

Roman street in the city of Caesarea in Israel.

THE ROMAN ART STYLES INFLUENCED OTHER CULTURES AS WELL

As the Roman Empire continued to expand across parts of Europe, Asia, and Africa, as it encircled the Mediterranean Sea, the citizens took their new blended art and architecture wherever they went. Roman statues as well as mosaics and buildings such as theatres and temples can be found at the location of Hadrian's Wall in northern England to North Africa's Leptis Magna, a prominent Roman city that was located in modern-day Libya.

From east to west, the influence of their art can be seen as far east as Constantinople to the location of the colony of Emerita Augusta on the west side of Spain.

Segovia, Spain Aqueduct.

When barbarian tribes overtook the empire, they kept some of their own art and cultural traditions, but they admired the Roman culture. They followed the same process the Romans had earlier by absorbing and transforming the Roman styles and techniques into their own culture.

The greatest revival of art from ancient Roman times was during the Italian Renaissance beginning in the 1300s, as the humanist movement took Italy out of the Middle Ages. The Renaissance elevated Roman art to the status of having a long-lasting legacy on the world's art traditions. You can still see its influence in every area of art.

A Roman sculpture lying in the Vatican Museums in Rome.

ROMAN SCULPTURE

Roman sculpture was an important part of every phase of daily life in the Roman Empire. Sculptures took many forms and decorated the Romans' private homes with their accompanying gardens, public and government buildings, and public parks. Roman architecture was adorned with sculpture. Sometimes Greek-style columns were added to buildings just for decoration and didn't support any of the building's weight. They often had no practical reason, but were simply added to the building for show.

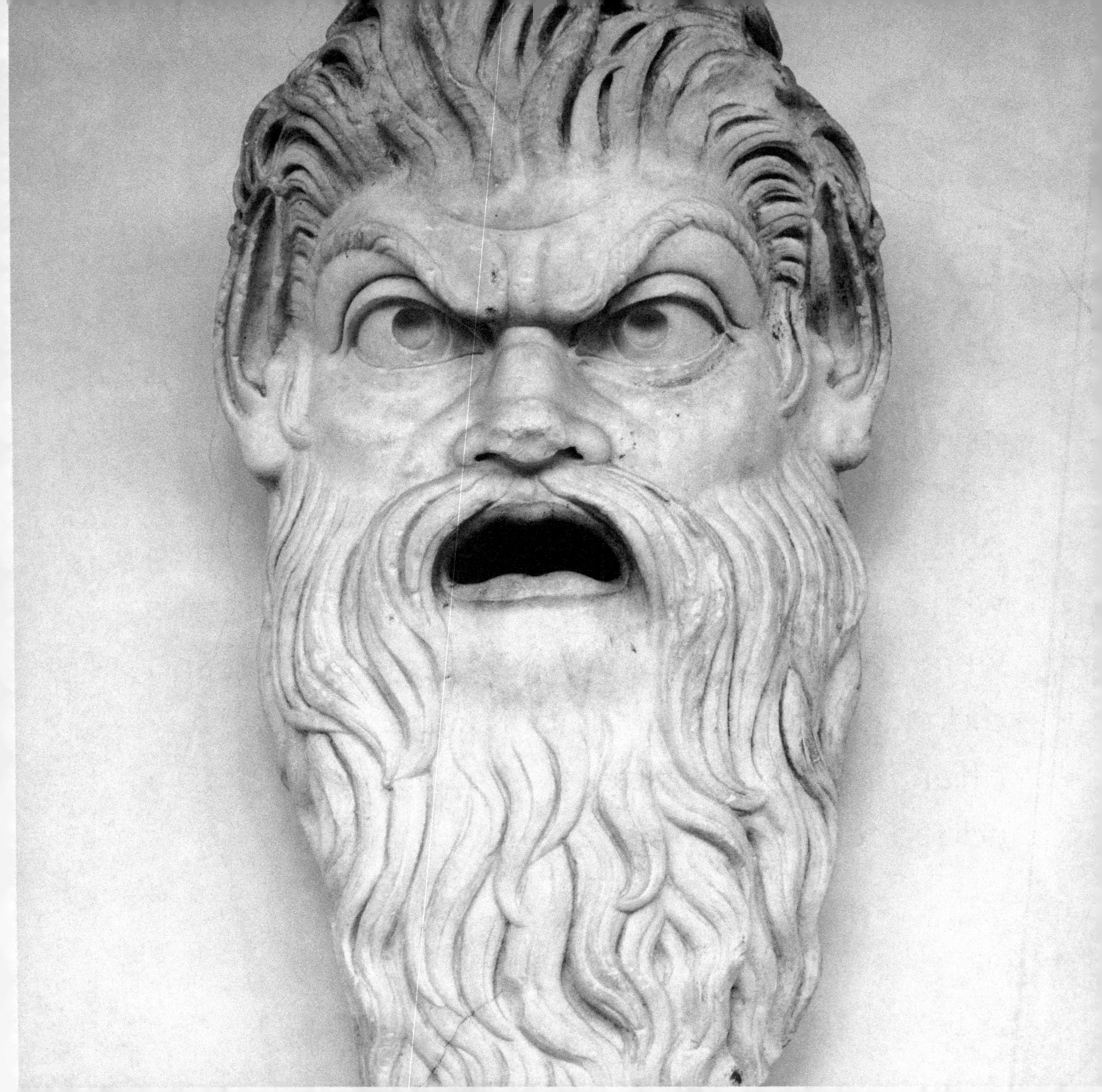

The Romans liberally copied Greek sculptures down to the last detail in some cases. In fact, this is how we know some of the Greek sculptures today through their Roman copies.

Types of sculptures included:

- Life-size statues of ancestors, gods or goddesses, famous philosophers, well known athletes, and victorious generals

- Portrait busts, sometimes just the head or the head and shoulders

Sculptures of Roman theater masks in the Baths of Diocletian.

- Reliefs, which were sculptures that were an integral part of a wall

- Sarcophagi, which are sculptures specifically created for tombs

One major difference in Greek versus Roman sculpture is that the Greeks made their sculptures perfect. They idealized the human body and didn't show any of its flaws. They wanted all their sculptures to look like perfect gods and goddesses.

The Romans, however, did show crooked noses, double chins, and balding heads in their bust portraits and life-size figures of emperors and famous military figures.

In ancient Rome, sculptures reached a huge peak of popularity. In fact, they became so popular that the poor overworked artists would crank out bodies without heads. Once an order was received for a specific person they would quickly finish the head and add it to the rest of the sculpture's body. Their skillful deception was rarely discovered.

Roman Emperors loved to have hundreds of statues made to honor themselves. They made sure these statues were placed throughout the city so that people would remember where the power seat was and not forget the emperor's many victorious battles.

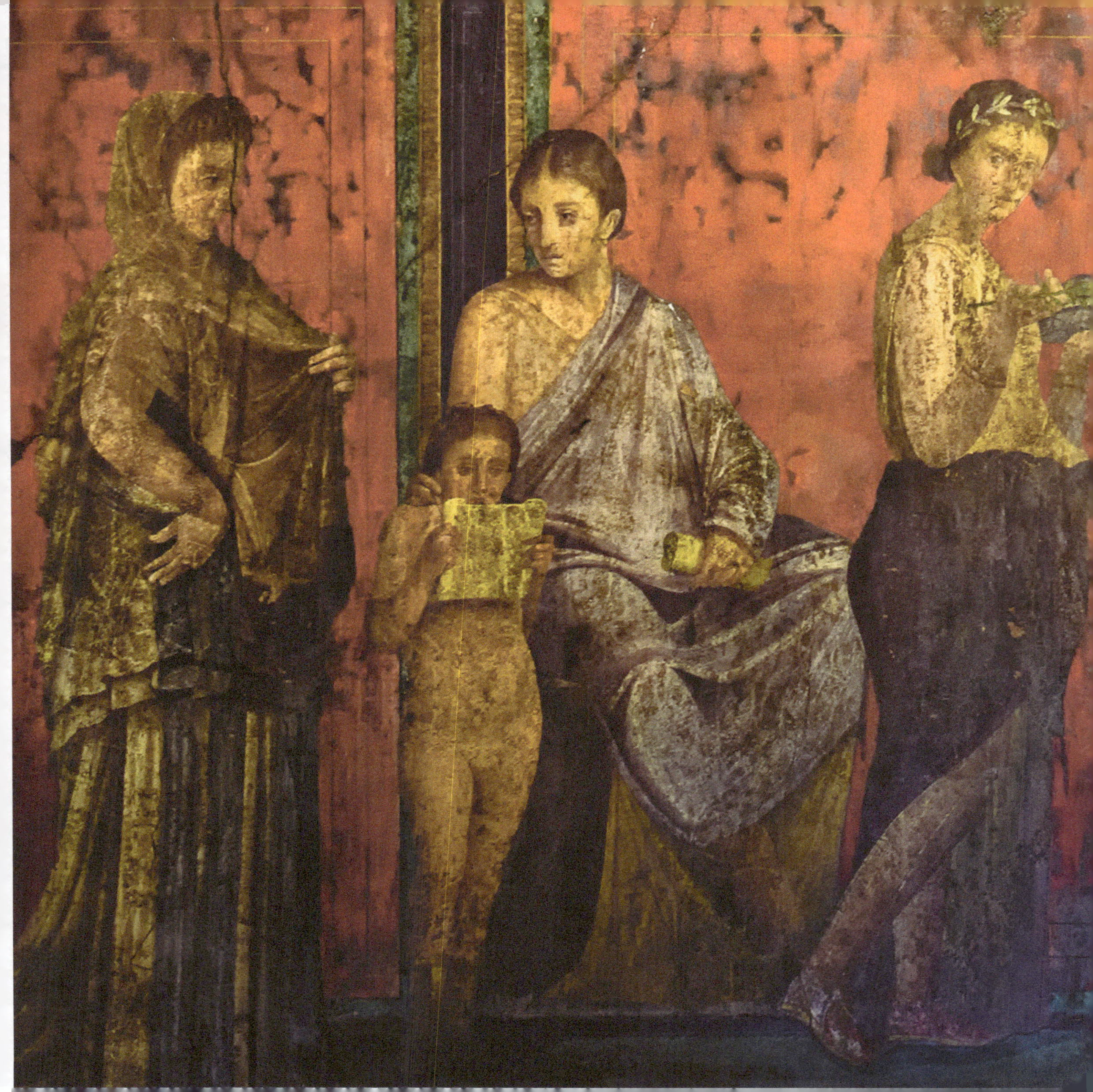

Dionysiac frieze, Villa of Mysteries, Pompeii.

ANCIENT ROMAN PAINTINGS

In the year 79 AD, the eruption of Mount Vesuvius covered the Italian city of Popeii with a layer of thick volcanic ash. Two thousand people died because they had stayed in the city. Centuries later, archaeologists were amazed to find much of the city preserved under the ash. The paintings that remain provided the information we know about Roman styles of painting today.

Paintings in Pompeii were primarily for decoration. Frescoes, which were paintings on wet plaster, were created on a house's inside walls to make the room appear larger or give the illusion of more depth, just as a mirror does. Often these were beautiful landscapes to give the homeowners something lovely to view since they had no window or view from their homes.

Roman fresco of a woman.

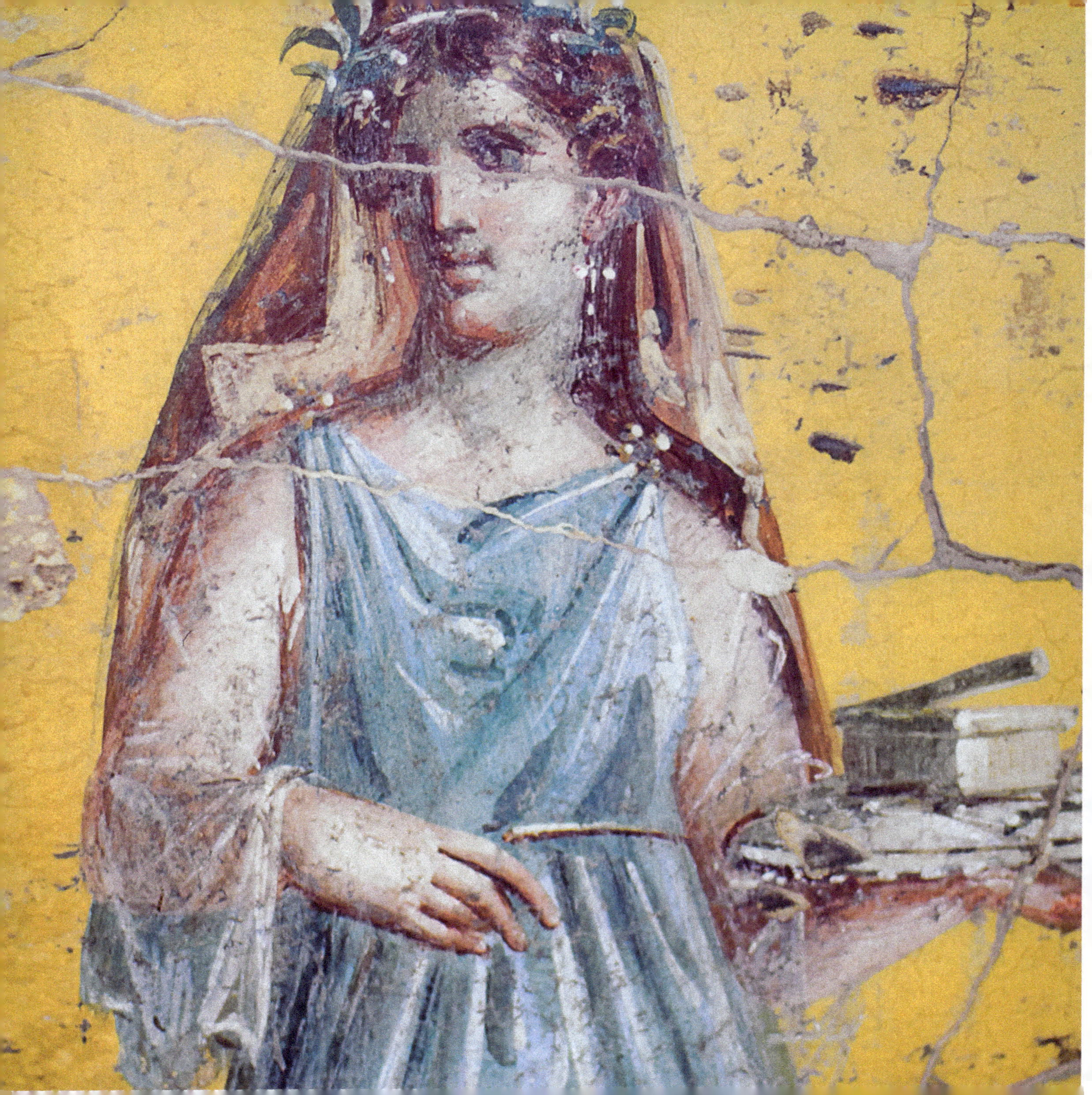

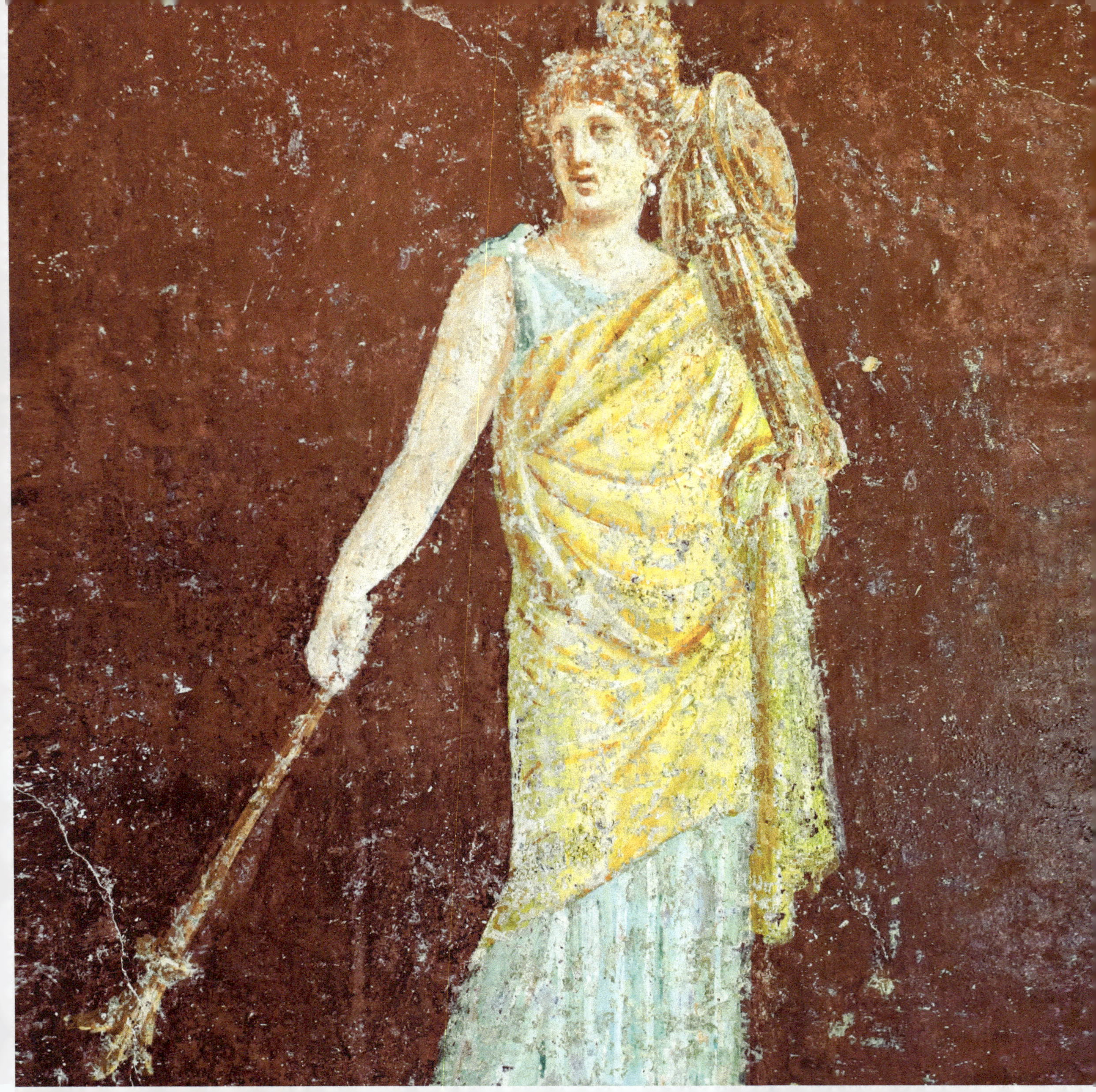

Columns and other architectural structures were often painted into the painting's scenes to give it depth or to frame it. The Roman artists were skillful in giving the illusion of perspective in their paintings. They used areas of tone and shading to add depth as well. Cream white, black, and red were popular paint colors that added drama and contrast to the paintings.

Fresco of the God Mercury.

Another technique the Romans used was to make mosaics from different colored tiles. It's thought that the Romans copied the Babylonian use of mosaics. Many mosaics have survived since ancient times and still retain their amazing original colors. They are so beautifully done that they often look like paintings from a distance. They were used as wall decorations and also as elaborate flooring.

Fresco house in Pompeii

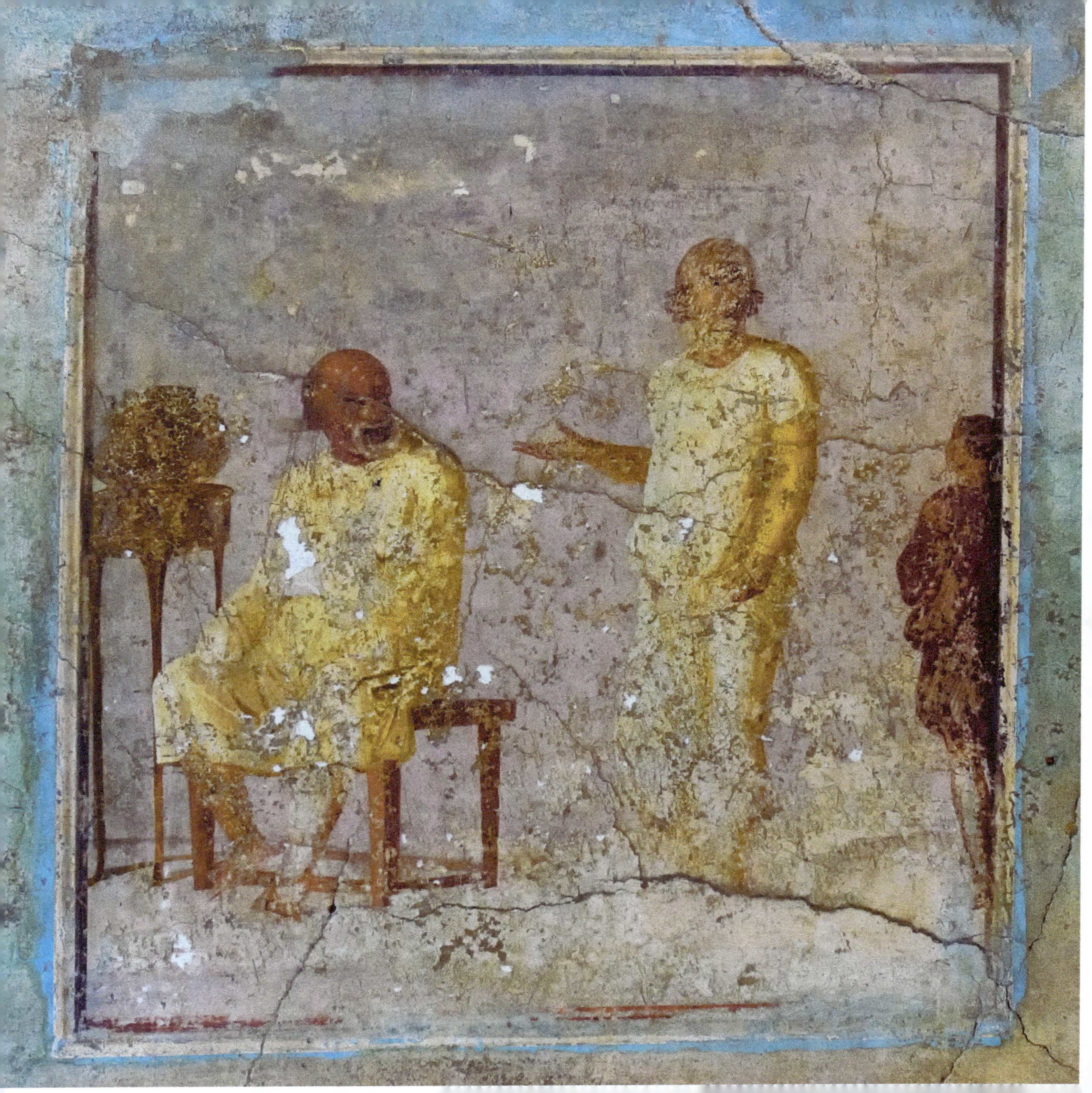

At times, the tiles were put together on site, but artists often created the tiles and the mosaic's base in the workshop and then brought them to the location for installation.

There were several different styles of mosaics:

- **OPUS SECTILE MOSAICS** had varying, specially-cut geometric shapes of marble, glass, and mother of pearl that were put together to get a specific design.

- **OPUS TESSELLATUM MOSAICS** were made of small cubes made of stone, marble, glass, or ceramic called tesserae and were generally arranged in straight lines to be used for floor decoration.

Mosaic floor opus tessellatum detail Gorgon.

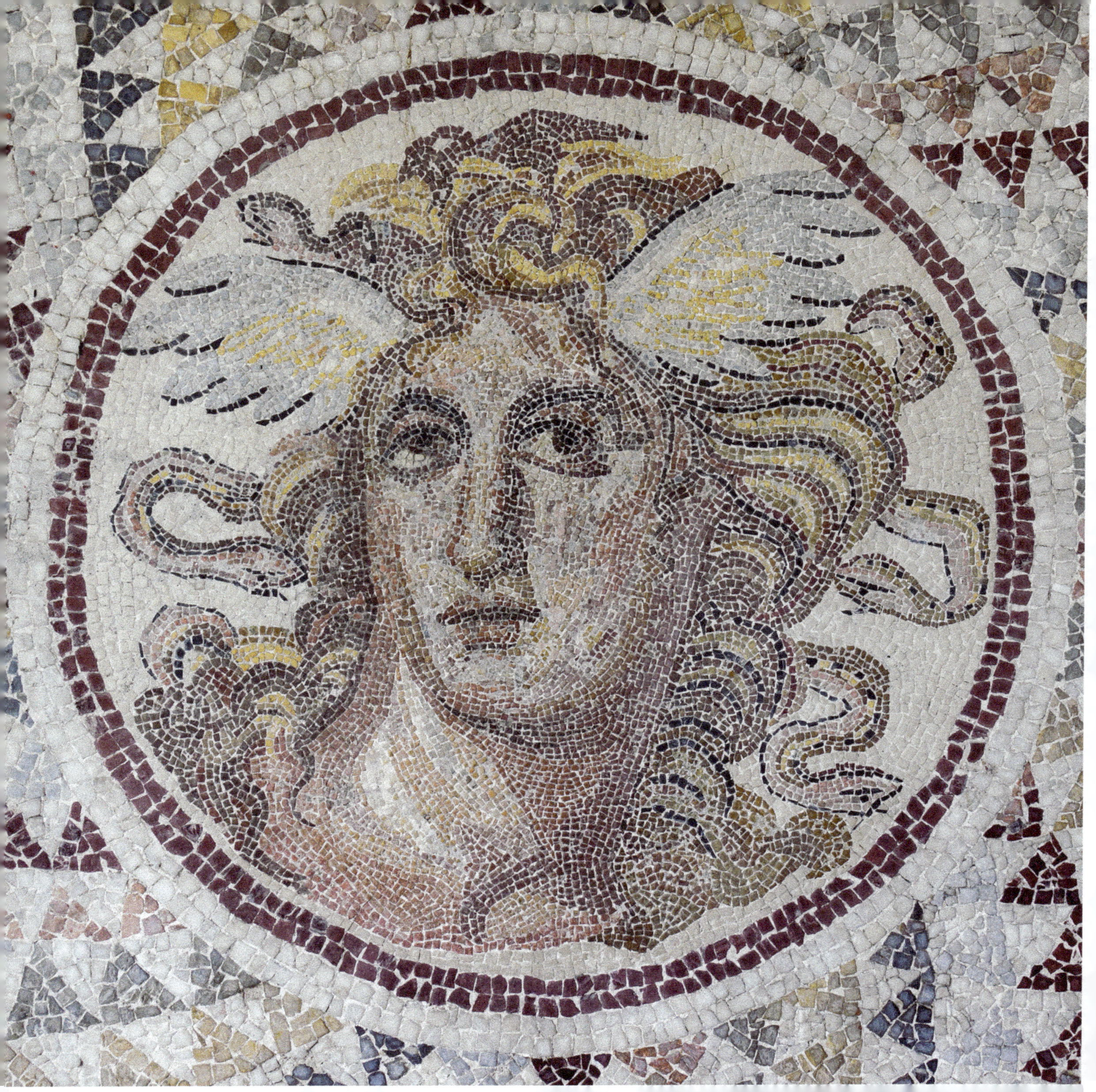

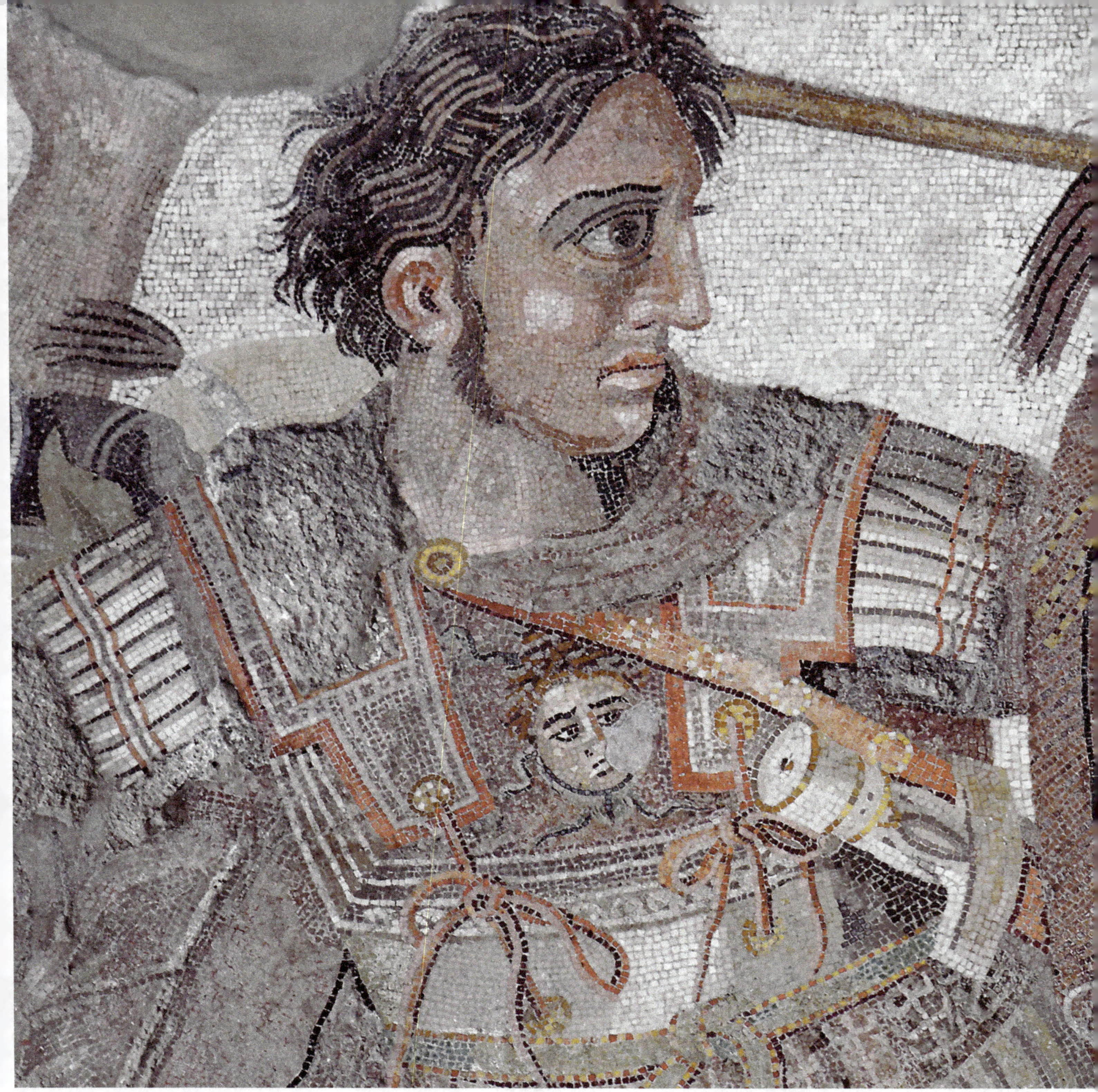

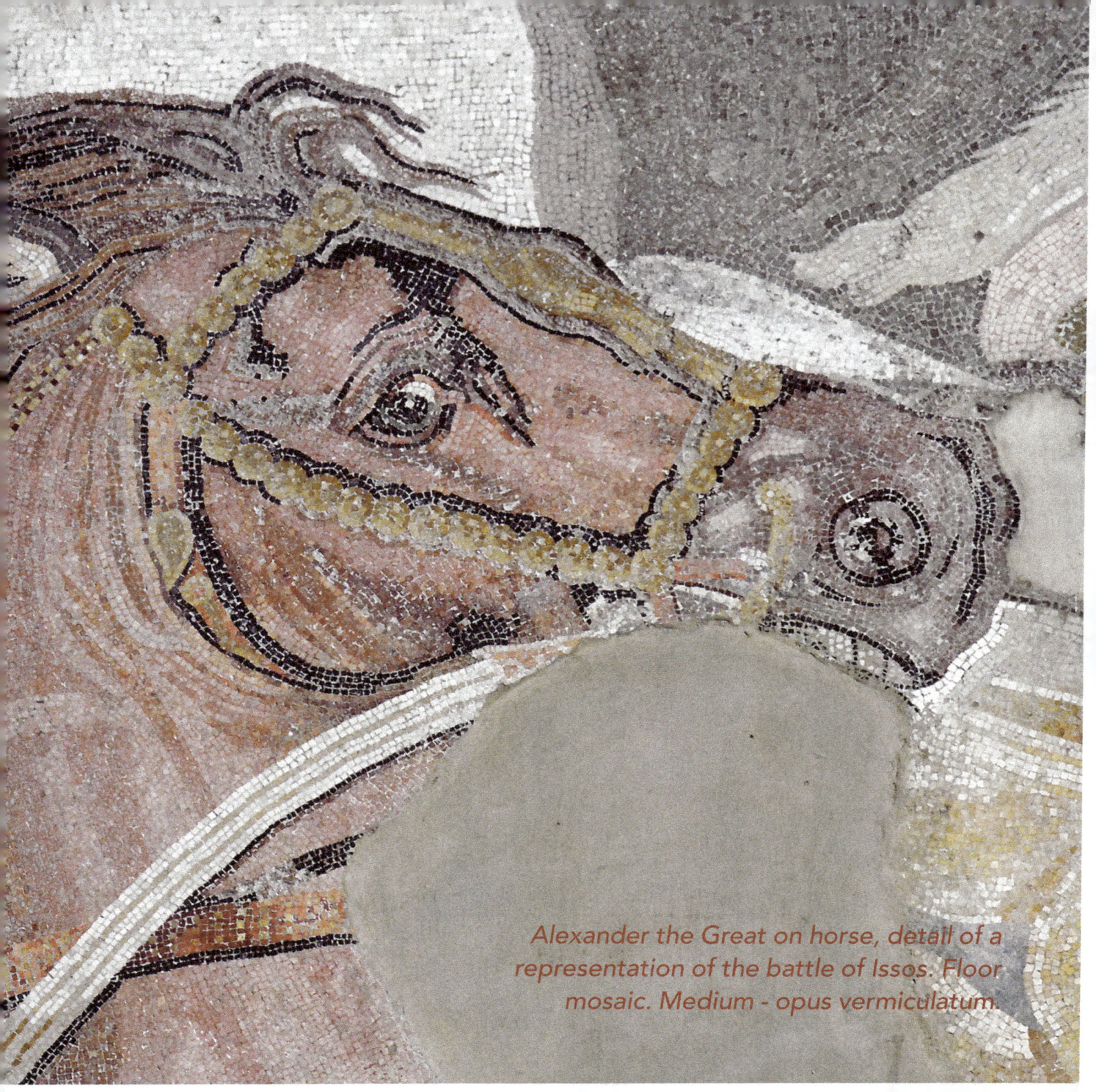

Alexander the Great on horse, detail of a representation of the battle of Issos. Floor mosaic. Medium - opus vermiculatum.

- **OPUS VERMICULATUM** were made of tesserae of different sizes that were used to make scenes and figures, which usually had clear outlines that curved around the design

Awesome! Now you know more about the art of Ancient Roman civilization. You can find more Art books from Baby Professor by searching the website of your favorite book retailer.

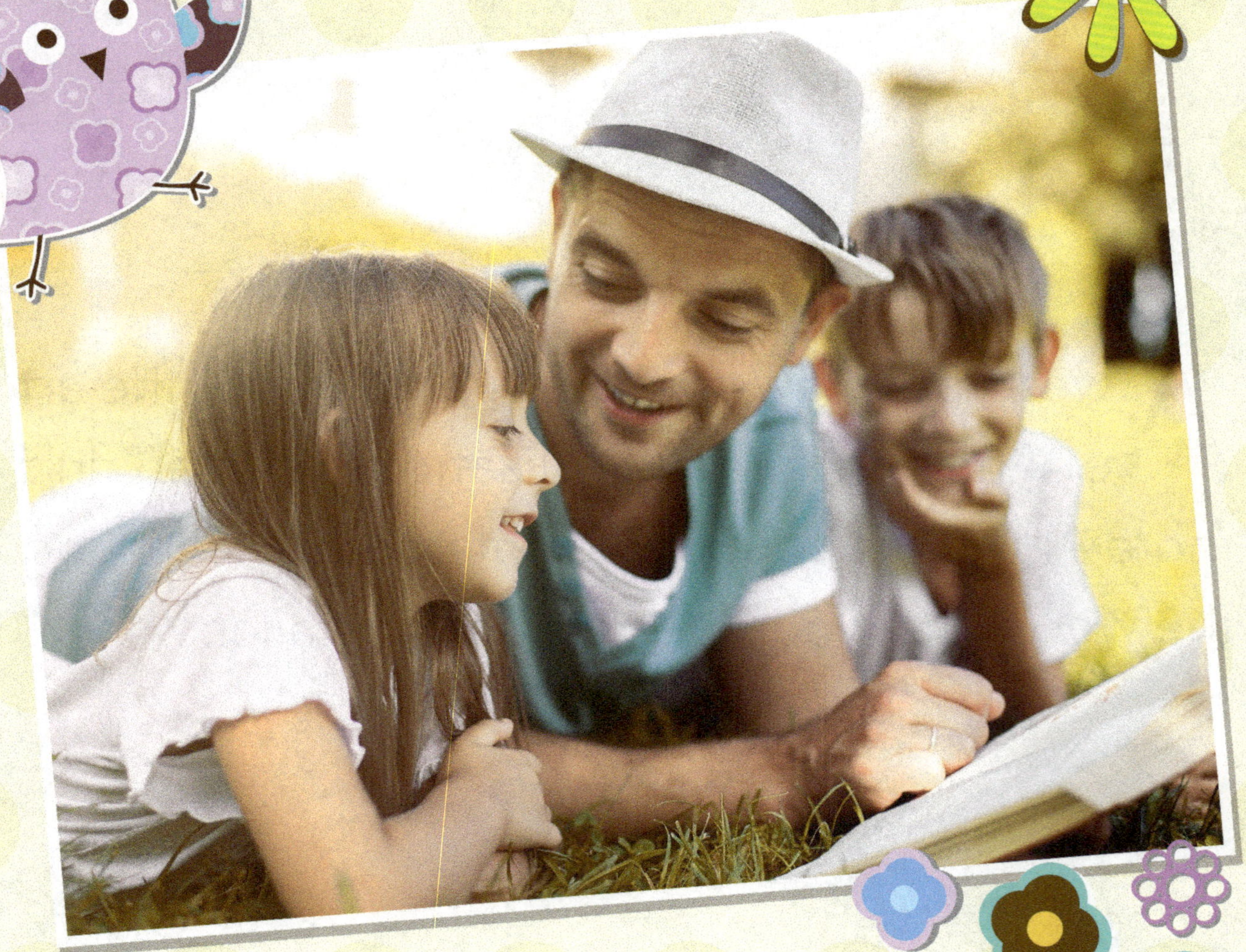

Visit

BABY PROFESSOR
EDUCATION KIDS

www.BabyProfessorBooks.com

to download Free Baby Professor eBooks and view our catalog of new and exciting Children's Books